MW01256887

Hotseat

for people who face tough questions

a handbook

Allan Campo

2012

Table of Contents:

IMPORTANT:

If you are reading this book as part of preparation for testimony in a legal proceeding, take care not to make any notes in the book. If you make notes, the notes may be treated as evidence in the case, and you could be required to provide a copy of them to the attorney(s) representing other parties in the case — including those whose interests are opposed to your own.

Introduction

Sooner or later, almost everyone ends up in the hotseat. People find themselves in a spot where they must answer questions under pressure, communicating with specificity and in great detail. Sometimes they are under legal or media scrutiny and are surprised to discover themselves feeling defensive, even if they haven't done anything wrong.

The settings where the questions are asked are often unfamiliar, and sometimes there is an audience. Addressing and handling inquiries in public can be stressful if you haven't done it much. Being the "designated explainer" in almost any setting carries heavy responsibilities. The hotseat truly can be "hot"!

Communicating from the hotseat is never ordinary conversation. It requires that you apply strict discipline to your listening and your speech so that there are no misstatements and no misunderstandings. There can be no guessing or assuming or generalities or casual comments. When you are in this position, you cannot go by the standards of ordinary spoken communication. You have to go by higher rules that are similar to giving testimony in a court of law. You will need to be able to make carefully considered, precise, and absolutely accurate answers to challenging questions.

If you were looking for a book about how to "spin," this isn't it. Spin is merely saying things that sound good. Spin is about putting actions or events in a light favorable to you or unfavorable to others, often without much reference to reality. Since spin isn't about truth and accuracy, it rarely survives close examination. Spin doesn't work very well for people in the hotseat. They need "anti-spin," the truth told so well and so clearly that it stands tall and strong. If you want to be able to tell the truth in that way, if you want to stand tall and strong, then this book will help.

Being in the hotseat may turn out to be a bit harder than expected. This is true for several reasons. The main reason is that, usually, you are obliged to communicate in a question-and-answer format and are rarely in a position to simply make a speech or relate a story. The truth must be communicated in the form of specific answers to specific questions. Occasionally, that makes the exchange of information awkward or even confusing. It can also be tedious.

If you are expecting to be asked some tough questions with regard to an issue or situation, if you are scheduled to be in the hotseat, there is a chance you are anxious about it. The stakes are sometimes very high. You may be concerned that you will make a misstatement or forget to cover something important. The fear of saying something completely wrong and getting in trouble for it is common, and you may be feeling some of that. The prospect of facing a forceful questioner may be bothering you. You may be worried about disappointing others or embarrassing them. You may be worried about embarrassing yourself, too. These forces can make the job seem even more challenging.

If you are feeling any of these emotions, you are not alone. In fact, most people experience similar anxieties when asked to represent their group or company in public, to speak to the press, or to give legal testimony.

When this little book was in draft, some of my colleagues wanted to call it "The Truth Book."

They said, "You tell us over and over that it is the truth that makes a speaker strong. You tell us that the more clearly a speaker can state the truth, the more powerful his message is. And you tell us that it is not telling the truth that it is the greatest challenge. It is defending the truth you have told."

I ultimately elected to call it "Hotseat" because I believe the term captures the core truth of what the book is really about. It is not a book of philosophy; it is a skill-building book. The book presumes you are intending to communicate with honesty and integrity, and then teaches you some of what you must know in order to do just that. It is designed to make your experience in the hotseat easier by instructing you in the essentials of communicating with precision and power, as though you are not merely answering questions, but giving testimony. Read it more than once. Try the simple exercises. You will like the results you get.

Why This Book?

"I'm just going to go in there and tell the truth. How hard can that be?" Why would a person need to read a book, then study and practice in order to do something as simple as that?

"Telling the truth" with clarity and precision actually demands a special style of communication. It occurs under unique conditions. Too many people have gone into hotseat settings armed with the best of intentions and a determination to "just speak the truth" or to "just tell it like it is," only to have great difficulty doing it successfully. Their words are misunderstood. They make misstatements. They get confused. They haven't thought systematically about the material they'll be asked to address or the questions they are likely to be asked. They are not fully prepared for the careful questioning they encounter.

Certain circumstances in our lives require extremely accurate and precisely honest spoken communication. Serving as a witness in a legal proceeding is one, as is serving as a corporate or government spokesperson. But there are others, of course. As you learn this material, you may find yourself applying the lessons in negotiations, in meetings with business colleagues, or in serious talks with family members.

The focus of this book is perhaps more upon questions than answers, and you will soon come to understand why that is so. The questions you will face are not ordinary requests for information or confirmation of facts. They are different. They are the questions that are likely to be asked of you by a professional questioner; an attorney or news reporter, for example. Such people are skilled in the construction of questions. Make no mistake about it; a trained questioner can absolutely grill an un-trained and under-prepared person who is unlucky enough to be in the hotseat. Study this book and apply the practices taught here and you will be ready for such situations.

Many of the most important lessons covered here will come from the universe of legal testi-mony, where the stakes are often the highest. What are our guiding principles? How about "The Truth, the Whole Truth, and Nothing but the Truth"?

The Truth

This may come as a surprise: telling the absolute truth for fifteen minutes could require hours of thoughtful preparation. You will find that you need to take time to think carefully about how to make precise descriptions and fully understandable statements. Accuracy in reporting the facts is essential. But accuracy is only the beginning.

The Whole Truth

Context and background can be the key to communicating the truth with the "whole-ness" that is required. You will need to think about the background facts and contextual forces related to the issues about which you will be asked. Most people don't have much experience at carefully setting key events and issues into the proper context when discussing them. You will probably be asked at least some questions that require you to speak carefully and clearly to contextual issues, so you must be prepared.

Nothing but the Truth

The Truth becomes something else when even the tiniest bit of exaggeration or other falsity is attached. You should scrupulously avoid the temptation to paint any point of fact in brighter colors than it deserves. That is part of the meaning of the phrase "Nothing but the Truth."

On the other hand, you may encounter attempts to diminish or re-cast your knowledge or experience. Protecting the truth requires diligent effort and also involves dealing thoughtfully with opposing or contrary positions.

Defending your perspective frequently takes longer and draws more energy than delivering the information in the first place! You will need to think about the questions you are likely to be asked by others who don't know anything about you, who may mistrust your position, or who hold a different view.

Some questioners may even begin with the presupposition that you will be less than honest with them. Their questions may be quite challenging. I suggest that you try to imagine the various ways such questions might be worded. Next, consider how you might answer these questions and then test your thoughts aloud with someone you trust. You and your listener-helper want to be sure there is sufficient clarity in your language.

Don't turn the considering of questions into a rehearsal. Rehearsals involve memorized scripts. Even the absolute truth rings less authentically when it is delivered in a rote fashion. The preparation you must learn to do is not "rehearsing." It is harder than that. It is making sure that you can think and talk about the issues from multiple perspectives without losing track of your own clear sense for what is true. It is being able to say the truth more than one way without losing connection with the essence. It is staying true to the truth. Further, you will need to be just as clear and honest in your opposition to incorrect suggestions and inaccurate characterizations as you are in making your affirmative statements. It will take some effort to prepare to do this, but you will like how you feel.

TIP:

I hope I have not made this all sound too hard. Learning to communicate under pressure with grace and precision certainly takes some work, but you should not think that you can't learn how to do it! It seems hard because most of us haven't had to think about and communicate our knowledge of something in this unique way! Do you remember when riding a bicycle seemed "hard"?

Keep reading! If you use this book and work diligently on getting ready for your big moment, you will find it far less difficult to manage your time in the hotseat, and, more important, you will be far less anxious.

The Truth:
Getting It Right

"Telling" vs. "Testifying"

Don't be a "teller", be a "testifier". When you are in the role of a "testifier," such as being a witness in a lawsuit, you can't just "tell" about facts. You usually need to address them with great care. For most of us, "telling" someone about something is a pretty relaxed exercise, and we may use different words every time we relate a story. We may notice that we emphasize different elements of a story each time we repeat it. We are not falsifying or altering the truth; we are just being normal humans in normal conversations. It is okay to be a "teller" in a normal conversation, but such relaxed speech is inadequate in the higher-stakes assignments we are talking about here.

As a "teller" in ordinary speech, we are usually comfortable with descriptions of events (for example) that are somewhat general. We don't feel a need to choose our words carefully in order to sharpen each point and refine each description into perfect focus. Being in the hotseat, whether giving testimony or answering challenging questions in some other setting, is not normal conversation. Being a "testifier" has tougher requirements. Precision and accuracy are the most important.

Precise Words

Some words and phrases are precise in their meaning, while others are not. For example, "accident" is not very precise. "Scaffolding collapse" is more precise.

"I saw the accident."

"I saw the scaffolding collapse."

Those statements are both true, but the second one conveys more information because it is more precise and addresses exactly what you saw. Your knowledge—your truth—is based on what you saw and heard and felt and thought. Your testimony, in the sense we use here, is the words you use to speak to your knowledge, to explain it. Others may have seen and heard and felt and thought something different, even at the same place and time. Their sense of the truth may be different, and their words probably will be different, too. That is to be expected, so you shouldn't be discouraged if you think that others may not describe something the same way you would. What is important is to understand and feel confident in the truth of your own experience. Further, only you can decide which words or phrases most accurately capture and communicate it.

If you are preparing for some time in the hot-seat, your job is to find and use the right words to convey what you know. You should be thinking today about the specific words you will use tomorrow. If you can't quite come up with the correct descriptive words, don't be afraid to use a dictionary or thesaurus! You are probably not an English teacher or a professional writer. You probably do not have years of experience describing things with precision so that people can fully understand them.

Think about this example: You are preparing to be asked questions about an exchange you had with another person during which you expressed some negative opinions about that person's actions.

What word might best capture the truth about your state of mind at the time?

Were you angry about something that the person did? Were you perhaps not entirely angry, but somewhat irritated instead, which to you is different? Or, were you feeling something stronger than mere anger, as you define the word? Perhaps you were outraged? Alternatively, might it be that you were feeling a combination of feelings, that you felt disappointed, let down, insulted or possibly disrespected? Could it be that you were feeling frustrated, actually, or exasperated?

Do you get the point that you should think carefully about the words you use to describe your experiences? Ask yourself what is the precise truth? What is the precise language that will express it?

Pick and Stick

One of my colleagues often tells witnesses that they should "pick and stick". He means that once they pick the correct language to convey the clearest sense of the truth, they should stick with that language. Pick the key descriptive words that speak to the truth with accuracy and precision, then stick with the use of those words. Don't give them up.

To succeed in this assignment, you will learn that you must bind yourself very tightly to the truth. Commit yourself to it. Then commit yourself to the best possible word selection that will get that truth across clearly to a critical audience who may, literally, be a judge and jury. The truth lives in the language you choose to express it. You'll learn later in this book that questioners may work very hard to get you to use their language to address an issue or event. Generally, you will want to oppose this. Small language shifts can kill the essence of the truth you want to express.

Don't Assume You Can Explain

Many people who are preparing to answer questions from the hotseat make a potentially serious mistake. They wrongly believe that knowing how to do something means that they can explain how to do it. Knowing how and explaining how are very different. You should not casually assume that you can clearly explain even simple aspects of the topics about which you will be asked.

Your knowledge about the many areas of your life is stored in numerous and quite varied forms in your brain. Retrieving that knowledge in the unique context of answering questions, often under pressure, can be surprisingly difficult. Sometimes people with extraordinary troves of knowledge can't find key information at all when asked questions outside the context within which they usually operate. They simply have never had to go inside their brain and try to find and describe the thing asked about. They use their knowledge in a unique context, in a laboratory, for example. To them the knowledge is simply there. When they need it, it is available!

What is really going on is that their retrieval of the information they need is only stimulated in their laboratory environment. Outside of that context, though, they usually don't need to retrieve the information and, unless they train others, they have never had to explain it to anyone outside of the laboratory! It can be challenging, indeed.

When a person in this circumstance is asked questions about technical aspects of his work while in a setting far away from the laboratory, it may take some time and careful thought to retrieve the correct information. Once he does find it, then he has to find words to accurately and truthfully speak to it. Finding the right words might not come all that easily. This is especially important in the hotseat, because the audience most likely will not have the same familiarity with the subject matter that the speaker's audience would have at work. With the untrained audience comes a need to use words that not only communicate the concepts accurately but in a way that makes sense to the listener.

You probably will need to build new "retrieval pathways" so that you can find and discuss your knowledge in a new setting and with appropriate language for the audience. There's only one way to do that pathway-building, that is to practice answering questions. Remember, you should not rehearse or memorize answers. What you need to do is get that information organized so that you can get to it and speak to it when you are asked about it. Thinking about the truth. Talking about it. Answering questions about it. Searching for more and more precise, accurate, and complete language to express it. That will help your brain organize it and retrieve it when you need it.

Find out for yourself. Get someone to ask you lots of questions about your work or about a principal interest area, such as a hobby. Think carefully about how to answer. Think especially about the key words you will use to name and describe things. Make the words precise. If you are like most people, you will notice elements that you can't explain very well at first. You have to work harder on those, searching for that precise language. Always, always, try to be precise when speaking to the truth.

Search Terms Help to Create Retrieval Pathways

You probably have tried to find information on the internet or in the memory of a computer by using key words as "search terms". Search terms are unique words or groups of words that "guide" the computer to the information you are seeking. The more general the search term, the wider the range of material that will be found. (Try doing an internet search for "beaches", for example.) More unique and specific search terms usually produce more unique and specific results. (Now, try doing an internet search for "pink sand beaches".)

The key words that you use repeatedly to describe the most important elements of the truth will begin to function for your brain in the same way that search terms function in a computer. And, just like on the internet, the more frequently the search terms are used, the more quickly the useful information appears at the top of the page! Further, more specific search terms that you use in your head will get you better and more detailed information from your memory, just as on the internet. The search terms have become the keys that open up the retrieval pathways. Your knowledge will be accessible anytime you need it.

Get those specific words right. Exactly right. Then, keep using them. They are the truth.

TIP:

A useful idea to understand is that there is fre-quently a significant difference between the objective truth (an empirically verifiable phenomenon) and sub-jective truth (what a particular person experiences and believes). Sometimes the two truths seem very different. While you may have some confidence that you know what is objectively true, you can only speak with cer-tainty to your own subjective truth.

Precise Statements

A big step toward success in the hotseat is learning how to make statements that have a high level of precision. Careful word selection is the foundation, but the accurate words you worked so hard to find must then be placed into sentences that carry them effectively. This will require some extra attention. Remember, the goal is to speak accurately and understandably, with language specific enough to reduce the likelihood of being misunderstood.

In our daily interactions with others, we often communicate with little attention to the rules of grammar. We ramble along, speaking in all sorts of funny ways; using incomplete sentences, little broken-off phrases, interrupted sentences, parentheticals, and sometimes in compound and complex run-on statements that never end.

Read the following excerpt from ordinary, everyday speech (and try to listen with your mind's ear):

"So, I told him…hey you must be feeling better, that's good…like, everything is gonna be all right with that situation…I mean a bird in the hand, you know…when it all happens to you and you feel bad, it's easy to get down…."

Hard to figure out what the speaker is talking about? Of course it is! You don't know anything about the speaker or the person he's discussing.

Usually, when we know a speaker well, we are calmly working away as we listen to something like the above passage, inserting assumptions and informed guesses that fill in the blanks. We are listening, but we are also both consciously and subconsciously interpreting and theorizing about what the speaker means. We often know something about the subject matter ("that situation") of the speaker's story before we hear it. Our knowledge gives context and background which helps us form an understanding of what the speaker means.

Most of the time, we don't notice that all this work is going on in our brains as we listen because we are all accustomed to doing it. Unfortunately, we also frequently get some of the story wrong and never know it, especially when we don't know the speaker as well as we think, or when we over-estimate our knowledge of the topic being addressed.

When you find yourself communicating in settings in which the context and background of your statements is not well understood by your listeners, you have to make up for it, at least in part, by speaking very precisely about not only some key idea, but also about its context and background. This more complete approach to speech will reduce the amount of guessing the listeners have to do in order to make sense of what you say. We will talk more about how to communicate context and background in a later chapter.

Simplicity

When answering questions in a hotseat setting, try your best to speak in short, simple sentences - subject, verb, object - with only one or two characterizing (descriptive) words. Here's an example: Susan (subject) kissed (verb) Bob (object) passionately (descriptive).

This direct style of speech really works. It may sound awkward or boring to you, but your listeners will appreciate the clarity of your communication.

You will make very few misstatements, and the audience will not misunderstand. Forcing yourself to speak in short sentences in this way will help you to organize your mind, too. You will have to focus upon how to describe specific things in a clear fashion.

One Breath

A good rule of thumb is to limit any answer to one breath. For most of us, all we can say with only one breath are somewhere between twelve and twenty four words. Try it! Take a breath and read aloud from this paragraph, counting on your fingers as you go. Chances are that you will need to take a breath before you hit twenty words. Try to remember that feeling of needing to take a breath and start thinking of it as an opportunity to stop. Notice how the period at the end of a sentence creates an opportunity to take a breath. Is this a coincidence? No.

Gaps

You may notice at some point that there are small gaps in your memory or that there are key topic areas about which you actually have little knowledge. That is an important thing to recognize. After all, a gap in memory or in actual knowledge is part of the truth, too, and you may need to speak to it. Usually, you should not worry about these things, as they are normal for all humans. What you should not do is try to fill in with a guess or an assumption about something, unless you specifically explain that you're making a guess or an assumption. Do this in order to be sure that the listeners understand what you are doing.

One of the most powerful statements you can make from the hotseat is "I don't know." Listeners will respect a speaker who honestly points out the line over which he cannot cross. If you are in business, you probably have had a boss explain to you how important it is to acknowledge what you don't know. It adds credibility to your answer to the later questions, when you address what you do know.

TIP:

You will learn as you go through this book that a key to precise communication is careful listening. Try going through some questions (about anything!) with a friend or business colleague, answering them in testifier mode: a strict subject, verb, object fashion. Listen to the question carefully. Then listen to yourself as you answer. Notice how clearly the information comes out and how strong it sounds and feels to say it in this simple way:

Q: "How'd you get to work today — drive your car?"

A: "Yes, I drove my car to the office."

Precise Limits

Did you know that many of us say things as truth in ordinary conversation that we could never "swear to"? Our spoken exchanges with friends or family often include the communication of beliefs, judgments, assumptions, guesses, theories, gossip, unverified stories from others, and information we get from the newspapers or television, all presented as truth. Unfortunately, none of those things meets the strict test of truth. Why? Because we do not actually know these things. We may believe them or treat them as truth, but that is not the same as being the truth.

For you to have full confidence that something about which you speak is absolutely true, you usually have to be the original source of the information. You saw it. You felt it. You heard it. You did it. You said it. Otherwise, it's just something you heard about or read about or (worst of all) guessed.

When in the hotseat, you should mark this line very boldly in the sand and not allow yourself to cross it. Put very precise limits on your statements. If you saw it, you know it. If you didn't see it, you concluded it. The two things are as different as the sun and the moon.

You should think about what you are to discuss and challenge yourself. How much do you truly know?

Lies and More Lies

Once, in order to make the point about precision and accuracy, I created a real-life example from the remarks of a colleague. She had just finished telling me about her day.

"I got to the office and Bob was in a bad mood. The copier down in Administration was on the blink and they were behind on a project. Then I went to a sales meeting and learned that our division is slipping behind projections. It's been a bad day."

I pointed out to her that although she was speaking casually, of course, she had probably said several things that might well be called "lies".

Let's analyze it: She probably did get to the office, so that part is okay. However, she has no idea if Bob was really "in a bad mood". She only knows that she concluded he was in a bad mood because of something he told her or the way he acted. She can't say for certain what his mood was!

Asked about how she knew "the copier was on the blink", she reported that someone (she can't remember who) said something about it having a problem. Further, nobody actually told her they were "behind on a project". She concluded that, too, because she believed they were at a point in the project where making copies was required. So, she put two-and-two together.

The sales meeting part of her story presented similar accuracy problems. She may well be right about all of it – but she doesn't actually know. She could never "testify" to anything but her guesses and conclusions. Anything else would be simply untrue.

This kind of rigorous analysis is just what you should do with regard to things about which you may be questioned. Do you really know it?

You Are Not a Mind Reader

Think about any commentary you may need to make with regard to the actions of another. Did you know that you have absolutely no idea why other people do what they do? You only know what someone *tells* you about why he did something. You only know what you guess about why he did something. You cannot actually know what he was thinking because you can't see into his mind. You cannot hear his thoughts. Don't fall into the trap of explaining the opinions or behavior of others from the witness stand or at the podium or at the conference table.

Putting precise limits on what you say is a way to "be true to the truth." Being careful in this way will make you a more trustworthy and believable communicator.

TIP:

Experienced communicators don't guess about other people while in the hotseat. You should learn to do the same. Think carefully about any comments you may need to make with regard to any particular person when answering questions. It is important to be thoughtful about this.

As a general rule, humans operate on a large number of assumptions about the other humans with whom they interact. Co-workers, for example, sometimes realize that they know very little about each other, even though they have worked together for years. What do you actually know about the background of others about whom you may be questioned? What do you really know about their education? What do you truly know about their beliefs with regard to the matters at hand?

The Whole Truth:
Telling the Complete Story

The Usefulness of Personal Background Information:

When another person tells us about something that happened to him, our sense of the meaning of that event is shaped by what we already know about that person and what we already know about the circumstances in which the event happened. Knowing the background and context of an event helps us understand the whole truth of another person's experience with that event.

Consider the following statement:

"The young man moved very slowly in response to the child's call for help."

If you knew that particular young man had a muscular disorder, you would have a very different reaction than somebody who didn't know about his disease.

Here's another:

Q. "You didn't read the directions for use on that lawnmower, did you?"

A. "No, I didn't read them."

Is this a negligent person who doesn't care enough about safety to read the directions? Not sure? What if you knew that the person above who "didn't read the directions" had been given thorough training on the use of that lawnmower by her father and was an expert at landscape work? You might have a different reaction than someone who didn't know that important background fact.

What we already know about someone helps us to see the true meaning of his behavior. Since we know that the decisions *we* make and the views *we* hold are strongly shaped by our background, we generally trust this way of measuring others. Most of us will go to this yardstick first when trying to figure out why a person did do this or didn't do that.

You may need to teach about elements of your own personal history in order for listeners to put together the complete picture, the whole truth, from your answers to certain questions. After learning something about your background and experiences, they will feel as though they know you. That helps them to understand your motivation and your perspective.

Identifying the relevant stuff in our background is easier said than done because we don't always know the elements of ourselves and our lives that give meaning to another's view of us.

At some point—and sooner is better than later—you should discuss this topic with someone who knows you well. Ask him how he would describe your personality to others. Listen carefully to the words he uses. Ask him what he thinks is important for people to know about you in order to understand who you are. Once again, listen carefully. It is worth the time and effort. And guess what? You may be in for a surprise or two when you learn how this other person would describe you!

TIP:

Do this exercise: Take just one hour to talk with someone who knows that you are going to be in the hotseat and who knows the topic to be covered but doesn't otherwise know much about your life.

Now, without talking about that topic at all, tell him/her a story that teaches about what your interests were as a child and what they are now. Tell the person about the most interesting experiences you have had over the course of your life. Are there any events that you believe helped to shape you into the kind of person you are? Tell that person the story of those experiences. Importantly, find out if some connection to your hotseat topic jumps into their mind while they are listening to you speak about yourself.

Here's another important point: Listen to yourself in the telling of these things about your life. You are likely to find that you are not really sure how to explain at least some of your own most precious interests or your most life-shaping experiences. Think about that! Many of us, perhaps most of us, are not that good at relating to others the key stories in our lives! That is usually because we haven't told these stories often, nor have we tried for absolute clarity when we did tell them. Get your listener to ask you questions until he/she completely understands this aspect of you — until the story is completely clear.

Are you noticing how much of this exercise is about listening?

Complete and Accurate Context Information

Context, according to our <u>New American Dictionary</u>, means "the circumstances that form the setting for an event, statement, or idea, and in terms of which it can be fully understood and assessed."

It is easy to misunderstand events if you don't understand the context in which they occur. Actually, it is context that gives events real meaning. A cup falls from a shelf. This should be no big deal, right? What if you knew it was Mary's great-grandmother's tea cup, the cup Great-grandmother Eleanor brought over from Ireland, the only possession Eleanor had? Now you understand the tears, the distress, the scale of Mary's loss.

A fact without context is like the shards of porcelain on the floor, perhaps barely noticed. But if you know Great-grandmother Eleanor's story, the shards on the floor might cause you to weep for Mary and her loss.

Here's an example from an interview that illustrates the impact of missing context:

Question: "It's true, isn't it, that there were three accidents at that plant in one year, and the safety procedures were still not updated?"

Answer: "Yes, that's true."

What in the world is this about? Did this person just admit that nobody was focused on these accidents? Is she acknowledging a deficient response to an obvious safety problem? Not sure? Of course, you're not sure! You don't know enough about this situation.

If a listener imagines three serious accidents, similar in the way they occurred, then he might start to think of this situation with some concern. But if he imagines minor accidents, each much different from the other, then he might land in a quite different place. He needs to know much more: Was anyone hurt? If so, how? When?

Remember, as people listen to you speak in response to any specific question, they are putting it into a bigger picture, already partly painted. They are inserting assumptions, making guesses, coming up with intuitive judgments about the complete truth so that it all fits together. This is not a conscious process. It is unconscious and natural as breathing. Your listeners cannot not do it. You make the job much easier for them when you give them accurate context information to use in the process. You are helping them get to the whole truth.

Here are some areas of personal context information that can often help listeners learn the whole truth from you about an event:

- Your health at the time in question.
- Your family's health and circumstances.
- Your mood and mindset at the time.
- What you had been doing just before the time in question.
- What you did just after that time.
- What else is going on in proximity to some event.
- What other people were nearby, involved or not.
- What was going on in the neighborhood, town, state, nation, world at the time.

Let's restate the above list as one of business or organizational context information that can help listeners understand the whole truth:

- The company's financial health at the time in question.
- The general circumstances of your company's industry at that time.
- The mood and mindset of management at the time.
- What was going on at the company just before the time in question.
- What the company did just after that time.
- What else is going on in business at that time.
- What businesses or government entities were located nearby, involved or not.
- What was going on in the neighborhood, town, state, nation, the world at the time.

Narrative

The richest form of context information is often called "story" or "narrative." The story behind an event puts the factual context into a vibrant framework of characters and conflicts, motives and goals, strife and resolution, and thus ties everything together in a way that gives the event its full meaning.

When explaining an event in normal conversation, we often say to others, "There's a story behind this that you have to know." This is the natural way that humans organize and explain the things that happen in their lives.

As you learn to speak about the context of things, you will become better and better at helping listeners understand the whole truth.

TIP:

The next time you watch or listen to the news, pay attention to the efficient way reporters get context information into stories. Usually it's the intro that sets that context and thus explains why the story is of interest. Compare these two introductions:

1: "In our next story, A Person walks Half a Mile to Borrow a Phone."

2: "In our next story, A Lone Blind Child Walks Half a Mile to Call 911."

Wow! That context information makes the story nearly irresistible, doesn't it? The simple fact that a person walked half a mile remains the same simple fact, of course. But that fact gets its real meaning from the context, the related facts that explain why it matters. Importantly, receiving the context "headline" first helps the listener prepare himself to absorb and understand the complete picture.

People who are frequently in the hotseat tend to spend a lot of time thinking about context "headlines" and how to say them clearly and concisely. They learn to introduce key answers to important questions in a style similar to that of newscasters.

Characterizing

One of the most important things you will work on in order to be a precise communicator is the accurate characterizing of the people, things, and events about which you must speak. When we talk about "characterizing" in testimony, we are talking about describing something in a way that captures its true nature and thus helps to explain what it really is. This language captures the important elements needed to understand the whole truth.

Three Ways to Characterize

There are three principal ways to characterize for the purpose of accurately conveying the truth:

Accurate Names

We have discussed the first a great deal already. You should be committed to the use of accurate names for objects or experiences that express the true nature of the object or experience. "I saw a bird flying above" is less precisely true than "I saw an eagle flying above." This precision actually gives more of the whole truth. Going from a general term, "bird", to a specific one, "eagle", makes an important difference. For most people, the experience of seeing an ordinary bird is different from that of seeing an eagle. If you want people to understand the moment, you have to capture it precisely.

Essential Descriptive Terms

The second element of characterization is the use of accurate and helpful descriptive terms that are essential to even more fully capture the truth. ("I saw an eagle flying above" will invoke a different experience for many listeners than "I saw an American eagle flying above."). By correctly naming the object, you have now brought the listener into an important emotional component of the experience. It was not just any large eagle; it was an American eagle. That characterization is an essential part of the whole truth.

Story

The third element of truthful characterization is the subject of this section. That is context, the story behind the mere fact, the narrative within which it exists. Knowing the context is necessary in order to understand the whole truth about an event.

"I saw an American eagle flying above" is closer to the truth than "I saw an eagle flying above". But, that, too, is less fully true than "As I was leaving my father's funeral, I saw an American eagle flying above." These descriptive words suggest a narrative and take us from our original statement to this one—from six words to fourteen. Going from an answer that takes a little over a second to speak to one that takes about three seconds completely changes the feel of the communication. It speaks to its essence, its truth. The fourteen-word sentence is an entire story in itself, full of pathos and symbolism. It is The Whole Truth.

Let's look at a more mundane example:

Question: "You threw away some documents the week before this event, didn't you?"

Answer: "Yes, ma'am, I did."

Hmmm. Is somebody "destroying the evidence"? Is this person trying to hide his guilt?

But this man doesn't feel guilty at all! That's because, during his first year of work for the company, he asked his boss about the company's practice of disposing of documents. His boss explained that if they didn't annually cull out the worthless file materials, the company would have to rent large warehouses just to store useless paper! "Keep what's important, his boss might say, but we must be sure to dispose of what is unnecessary."

Once our man knows the story, then he is prepared to truthfully and accurately characterize his actions as "our regular practice" and not as "throwing away documents," but "discarding unnecessary file materials." These are important distinctions, don't you agree?

Now, let's ask that question again:

Question: "You threw away some documents the week before this event, didn't you?"

Answer: "Yes, ma'am, it's our regular practice to discard unnecessary paper file materials."

It sounds different, doesn't it? Here the man includes in his brief answer the important context truth that it is (his company's) "regular practice" to "discard unnecessary file materials." Notice that he also re-characterizes the "documents" to a name he thinks is more accurate, terming them "file materials" instead. These refined characterizations matter a great deal, as they help to address the truth about his actions. He may have to explain further in follow up questions, but the basic message has been sent. The Whole Truth is being taught to the listener.

Story-telling

Much has been written about the power of storytelling in communication. Frequently, context explanations can best be given as short stories. In our earlier example, our man in the hotseat might very well have told the story of the conversation with his boss as a useful way to explain about "destroying documents".

In point of fact, almost all context explanation is narrative in form. That is, it tells some sort of story. One of the ways you will recognize when you are using powerful words to speak to the truth is when the words alone suggest rich background stories. Some words simply demand a story.

Q: "Mr. Smith, you didn't speak with anyone that day, did you?"

A: "That's right. I was feeling a lot of grief then, and it was keeping me pretty quiet."

"Grief"? The listener certainly wants to know what that is about! What's the story, here? Grief is something you feel because of a tragedy, usually a very personal one. Everyone knows about grief, understands the feelings, and empathizes in a great or small way. Words that are linked to universal human stories share this quality. They are reactions to an event of personal importance. Here are a few others:

- Triumph
- Regret
- Celebration
- Remorse
- Satisfaction
- Loss
- Resolution

These words could each stand as the title of an interesting story ("My Triumph"). When you use such a word in an answer to a question, the listener will want to know the rest of the story. The rest, of course, is the full context that teaches the complete truth of things, the whole truth that you want to tell.

TIP:

Think of an issue about which you may be asked and make a list of the people involved and the actions taken (or not taken). You are going to work on your characterizations of each. Accurate characterizations put people and events in the right light and thus help the listener understand the full truth about a situation.

Now, consider the first person on the list and address the "who, what, where, when, and why" with regard to him and his actions. Characterize a few of the "whos," then the "whats," then the "wheres," etc.

Here's an example: A sales representative recently lost a big client account.

Who: "A sales representative and a client" (Now characterize the people in a way that captures the truth about them.)

An "inexperienced sales representative" and a "very demanding" client.

What: "There was a disagreement with the sales representative." (Now characterize both the disagreement and the sales representative.)

An "unnecessary" disagreement between a "very demanding" client and "an inexperienced" sales representative.

Go on to the "where," "when, and "why" characterizations, continuing the pattern. Do you see how powerful appropriate characterizing terms can be?

Nothing but the Truth:
Defending Yourself, Your Colleagues, Your Company or Organization

The words you speak from the hotseat should meet the strict test of being nothing but the truth. What follows is a discussion of how to hold on to that truth and maintain a powerful and credible voice, even when under attack.

The two main settings we will look to for our lessons are giving testimony in a legal setting and serving as a spokesperson. The rules are far more similar than different, and each setting can serve to instruct the other. There is a lot to think about.

Being a Witness

Giving Deposition Testimony and Trial Testimony

Let's talk about legal testimony, about being a witness in a court case. Witnesses are likely to face two different kinds of questioning from opposing attorneys. The first of these are the questions asked in a deposition. A deposition is a kind of formal interview, usually at a lawyer's office.

First, the witness is required to answer questions from an opposing attorney about himself and what he knows with regard to the case. Then his attorney may ask some follow-up questions. He will be under oath to give only the truth, just as if he were in a courtroom. There will be a court reporter present, and the deposition may be videotaped. Depositions are very important, as they establish the basic facts of the case and affect what will or will not be the subject of the trial. A witness should prepare thoughtfully and thoroughly for a deposition.

Sometimes depositions are very long and tedious. One reason for this is that in a deposition an attorney can ask about virtually anything. For many reasons, much of what is covered in a deposition will never be asked about in the courtroom during a trial. However, during a deposition the questioning attorney may want to touch every subject he/she can think of in order to fully understand what the witness knows and can testify about.

The second kind of questioning a witness will face from an opposing attorney is called cross-examination. Cross-examination usually happens only in a courtroom during the trial of a case. Normally, the witness is cross-examined after he has made his direct testimony in the courtroom, carefully communicating the truth while being guided by questions from his attorney.

Cross-examination is usually less tedious and more to the point than the questioning witnesses face at a deposition, but it is often based in part upon earlier deposition testimony as well as the direct testimony that immediately precedes it.

If you are going to testify at trial, you should ask your attorney to help you prepare for cross-examination, as the judge and jury will be very interested in how you handle it.

Witness Preparation

Preparing to testify can be, as you have almost surely recognized by now, hard work. It is not enough to know what you know, believe what you believe, and remember what you remember. In order to testify, you have to deliver your knowledge, sincere beliefs, and memories, your truth, as clearly spoken communication that others can fully understand and apply to the matter at issue.

Your lawyer should be quite involved with you in thinking about and preparing your testimony. His first job is making sure that your testimony is relevant, that it appropriately bears upon the matter at hand. Witnesses often misunderstand what is actually relevant and may expect to testify about certain things only to learn that those things don't really apply to the issues in the case.

Here's an example: Jim is a supervisor at a small factory. Bob was a contractor doing specialized machine work on certain projects. Jim was present when Bob got his hand caught in a drill press and was seriously injured. Bob later sued the drill press manufacturer, claiming that the machine wasn't safely designed and that he wouldn't have been hurt if it had been done correctly. He also sued Jim's company, alleging that they knew or should have known that the machine wasn't safe. Jim is upset about these allegations, as they seem to him to suggest that he wasn't a good supervisor.

Jim shows up for his witness preparation and meets with the company's lawyer. Jim wants to testify about how good a supervisor he is, how much he cares about people, and how he would never let anyone be put in harm's way. These things are all true, of course, but they may not be relevant to what the company did or did not know about the safety of the drill press. Jim is hurt and offended by the lawsuit, but that is not the point. Jim's lawyer should encourage Jim to focus upon what is directly relevant: The drill press. The company's accident history. The safety program. How the company selects equipment.

The lawyer who works with you or who represents you should likewise be very engaged with you in the witness preparation meeting. Be ready for this: Your lawyer should have comments and opinions about your testimony. It is his job. He cannot and surely will not try to tell you what the truth is, but he can and should give you feedback on its relevance and how clearly and fully you express it.

Your job:

Testify to the truth.

Your attorney's job:

Make sure that what you testify about is relevant.

Give you feedback on the clarity of your testimony.

Give you feedback on the conciseness of your testimony.

Give you feedback on the completeness of your testimony.

In doing this job, the attorney will probably ask you to speak repeatedly to the material about which you are to be asked. He should ask you questions from various different perspectives, hopefully approaching topics from unexpected angles. We've discussed this before, and point it out again to you because it is an important and useful process. It helps you to crystallize your thinking and forces you to examine your memory for greater detail and more precision. You probably also can see that it aids you in developing those retrieval pathways also discussed earlier in this book.

Repetitive conversation with your attorney will help to reveal any potential for confusion in the wording you use to speak your truth. Remember, it loses its utility as truth if it can't be understood. Your testimony isn't helpful to a judge or jury if you can't convey it fully. It won't be the whole truth.

Another important function of the witness preparation meeting is that your lawyer will learn in great detail your truth and how you intend to tell it. This will help him to help you in the deposition if you get tired and have some kind of mental lapse and start getting simple things wrong. This happens to almost everyone at one point or another in testimony. Many very intelligent and sincere people have had a moment of mental fatigue when they called a blue car a yellow truck and referred to Mr. Jones as Mr. Johnson. Your lawyer, because he knows your truth backwards and forwards, will immediately recognize that this is happening and call for a break so that you can get a breather and re-group.

The witness preparation process also helps to get you ready for the most challenging part of testimony, being questioned by an attorney on the opposite side of the case. It is sometimes termed "adverse examination". Actually, the first testimony you give, at least in a civil case, is likely to be an adverse examination in a deposition.

The Rules for Adverse Examination

In general, the following are the rules when you are being examined by an attorney adverse to your side of the case:

- You must take an oath to speak only the truth.
- You may not refuse to answer a question (unless it would be legally improper to answer).
- The questioner decides what topics will be covered and in what order.

- The questioner decides how to structure the questions.
- The questioner decides what terms and characterizations to use in the questions.
- The questioner decides what, if any, propositions are built into the questions.

If you are answering questions in a news conference or as the designated spokesperson at a public hearing, you may wonder whether these rules will apply in those settings, too. The answer is that generally they will. Most reporters, for example, learn to ask questions in a planned order and will try to stick to it. Most also learn to insert provocative characterizations into questions, too, testing for your reactions. Questions asked of you at public hearings, no matter who asks them, will often have been authored in advance by attorneys. They will frequently have these same qualities.

The Toughest Obstacle: The Leading Question

Whether you are testifying as a witness, answering questions in a formal business meeting, or speaking with a reporter, you should prepare thoughtfully to defend the whole truth as you understand it. You will face some unique difficulties in this special communications situation. There are obstacles to be overcome in order for you to best defend your truth. Let's talk about what can be the most imposing obstacle in any hotseat situation: the "leading question."

Look at these two questions:

Q. 1: "Can you describe the accident?" (non-leading)

Q. 2: "The catastrophic accident in which you were involved was the result of a series of acts of negligence, wasn't it?" (leading)

Leading questions allow the questioner to test your reaction to an idea or proposition. The use of leading questions gives the questioner a great deal of power over the flow and content of the communication. Most of the rest of this handbook will deal with how you can manage your way through a variety of the issues that emerge when you are questioned by an attorney or other professional questioner. You will find that leading questions are their principal tool.

TIP:

Practice this drill with a friend or family member as a way to tune your ear to leading questions and the inaccuracies they frequently contain:

Get that person to ask you questions about something (anything!) you both know about, but he or she should use only leading questions. You could answer questions about a television program you both watched, a person you both know, or an incident you both experienced at work. Almost anything. You should listen to the questions carefully and correct any assumptions or characterizations with which you do not completely agree. This a manner of protecting the truth that is sometimes called "gatekeeping" (as in, guarding the gates of truth). At first it might seem awkward, acting as a gatekeeper in a conversation with a friend - but, go ahead and take a chance. This can be fun!

Leading questions are surprisingly easy to create. All your friend needs to do is make short or long statements that have a request for agreement tagged onto the end. How about some examples?

"X plus Y is Z – isn't that true?" "A minus B is C – don't you agree?" "Tall is different from short – that's correct isn't it?"

Get the picture?

Your conversation thus might sound like this:

Friend: "That was a great party last night, and even though you were tired, you enjoyed yourself completely, didn't you?"

Answer: "It was a great party, but I wasn't tired. I actually had a headache."

Friend: "I loved that navy colored outfit you had on. That cost quite a bit, didn't it?"

Answer: "Thank you, it was actually a black suit my sister gave me, so I don't know how much it cost."

Friend: "You are such a difficult person: you contradict almost everything I say, isn't that true!?"

Answer: "It is not being difficult if I correct you when you are getting the facts wrong."

Half of the art of precise communication is learning to listen carefully to questions. You should begin to focus upon the specific nouns and verbs and descriptive terms or phrases that are being used by the questioner. Force yourself to focus upon those words, filter them for accuracy, and then correct the ones that aren't precisely right, that aren't precisely accurate, and that aren't precisely true. When you are doing that, you are guarding the truth. You are being a gatekeeper.

Gatekeeping

Protecting the truth, what legal communications experts call "gatekeeping", can be more challenging than many witnesses expect. Gatekeeping is something most of us don't have to do very often. We are not often asked questions which are less inquiries for the truth than they are challenges to that truth. The questions you will get from an attorney adverse to you will often only *seem* to be questions. They are something else dressed up as a question. What these "questions" often are actually intended to do is serve as vehicles to persuade you to a different view of the facts, or, alternatively, to completely dissuade you (or the listener) from your sense of the truth.

Why it Seems Difficult

1) Thinking and word selection not crystallized.
2) Lack of question-management skill
3) Interference

The process is made more difficult if you still don't have a clearly formed sense of what the truth is and what precise words best express it. Your thinking really needs to *crystallize*! If you haven't thought about it enough and spoken about it enough with your attorney, then you will not have your brain exercised well enough that those key words and terms which best express your truth are easily retrieved. Fully-formed thoughts, "crystallized" ideas, are easy to pull up when you are asked about them. Getting that retrieval process reliably working is the first order of business.

The questioning may also seem difficult at first because you don't yet know how to manage poorly formed questions or questions designed to persuade or dissuade. *Managing* this type of question is where some measure of gatekeeping skill will help you to protect the truth as you understand it. There are a number of simple gatekeeping methods for handling these questions that can help. We will discuss gatekeeping a great deal in the upcoming pages.

A third source of difficulty, and one that is underestimated, is what is sometimes called *interference*. Perhaps you can recall a time when you heard buzzing and static in your cell phone because of electronic waves emitting from some nearby machine. That buzzing and static "interfered" with your cell phone signal. It was harder to communicate, wasn't it? If the noise was loud or the tone irritating, it may even have been hard to think. Interference "noise" can happen inside your head, also, when a thought is distracting you so much that you can't think very well. Interference is a common problem for witnesses during testimony, so there is much more to come on this topic.

Just Answer the Question

If you are briefed by an attorney prior to your testimony, you are apt to be advised to "just answer the question." This advice is very good, but it is inadequate unless fully explained. The advice really might be stated more completely as "just answer the question, *if* it is answerable."

You may recall that earlier you saw a listing of the rules for a deposition and one of them was that you may not refuse to answer a question. This is true, you cannot refuse to answer a legally allowable question. But, you absolutely should refuse to answer a question, even if it is legally allowable to ask, if you cannot answer because *there is something wrong with the question.* You are there to testify to the truth. If the question makes it impossible to do just that, it is unanswerable as asked and you should say so.

In our typical relaxed exchanges with others, a question or comment is voiced which stimulates us to react. Our reaction is spontaneous and we feel no need to get things precisely right. We neither require that the question be completely precise and understandable nor do we require absolute accuracy in our answer. We are not so much answering a question as thinking out loud about a topic. Unfortunately, that is a very bad practice for someone giving testimony.

Thinking out loud is often speculative, an experiment in how to speak about a topic. We don't usually expect to be held to an accounting for every word. When you give testimony, though, you will be held accountable for every word you say. But, there is another important element you must understand. You will also, in a way, be held accountable for the words used by the questioner.

If the questioner's words are inaccurate and you don't say so, you have essentially endorsed them as asked. You should treat a question with inaccuracies or error in its language as an unanswerable question and ask for another question that does not have those problems. Your attorney will protect your right to do this. Then, your answer should always be a direct response to the now-revised question, stated in the shortest and most precise way. That will help you hold to the truth and nothing but the truth.

Preventing yourself from answering a leading question in a "thinking out loud" fashion may be harder than you expect. Giving imprecise responses is more the rule than the exception, and you are likely to discover that you do it, as do we all, a great deal. However, you can learn to be better at making more accurate answers. It starts, as you have heard before, with listening to the question.

You will notice that a problem with trying to "just answer the question" is that the question is just not that easy to answer. Leading questions usually have more than one part and may present problems of complexity, awkwardness, poor word selection, inaccuracy, etc. Frequently, they are not completely inaccurate or erroneous, just hard to follow. In that instance you will need to know what to do. Much of what we talk about next will help you know what to do when you are entirely willing to answer a well-formed question with the whole truth, but aren't getting the chance to do so because there's something wrong with the question on the table.

Three Common Problems
- Questioning pace is too fast.
- Questions are too long.
- Questions are of the forced-choice "yes/no" type.

Too Fast: The single most common complaint made from the hotseat is that the questions are coming too fast. You will be trying to be thoughtful about every word. That is hard to do when the questions are coming at you machine-gun style.

Some attorneys, interviewers, and reporters ask rapid-fire questions intentionally, imagining that they can keep a testifier a little bit off balance using this classic interrogation technique. But it is a turn-off to many listeners, and the manipulation really provides little advantage, especially when the testifier does what you will do: simply ask the questioner to go more slowly.

The questioner in these settings has many advantages, but you should still have the right to think about the question and about the answer; that means the questions should be asked at a pace that you can follow. When you insist upon this very reasonable courtesy, you are helping yourself by reducing interference.

Rapidly paced questioning can leave questions and answers piling upon one another in your head, rippling through your mind like the criss-crossing waves on a pond after several stones have been tossed in, or like the echoes and feedback of electronic speakers placed too close together. This is *interference*. You need to have time to settle the waters and quiet the noise so that you can think clearly.

Questions Too Long: You should expect to have the right to an understandable question. If a questioner asks a long, convoluted question that seems to go on for days, you could misunderstand part of it, get mixed up, or not notice some mischaracterization in it. Since you have assumed the duty to ensure accuracy by taking an oath, you have the right to ask to have the question shortened. Here's the test: if you can't say it back exactly as asked, it's too long. At the very least, ask to have it repeated.

The biggest problem with long questions is that we usually can't hold them in mind in their entirety as we consider our response. Our brains will try to reduce the question to manageable scale by either simply dropping pieces of the question out, or by automatically re-phrasing it into something shorter, a self-generated summary of the question. There is a great deal of potential for error in this process, and you may suffer for it. You should not have to re-write the question for the questioner.

Forced-Choice: Forced-choice questions are questions that are designed to limit the options of the person who is to answer them. As the name implies, you have to make a decision. You are forced to choose, usually between two positions. Forced-choice questions have great utility in the worlds of science and mathematics and philosophy. For the same reasons, they also have some utility in other circumstances for testing the truth of a statement or the strength of a position, as they may compel clear thought and clear speech in both the person asking and the person answering. A proposition is framed as a question and you must accept or reject it, agree or disagree. That seems okay, doesn't it? But what happens in the real world?

What happens is that people in the hotseat get asked yes/no questions and just don't believe they can really be answered with a simple yes or no. Sometimes they are asked these questions and think the answer is something close to yes or close to no, but not always—not all the time. They don't know what to do because the questioner has only offered the two absolutes.

But you will know what to do. You will understand that you should not answer "yes" if the answer should actually be "most of the time — yes." Remember, your assignment is to tell the truth, to answer with accuracy. An absolute "yes" and "most of the time — yes" are very, very, different. That is the whole truth and nothing but the truth.

When it turns out that you just can't answer a question with a simple yes/no or an agree/disagree, you should say so because that is the truth. Do not be afraid that you will be seen as impolite or uncooperative. If you are sincerely trying to get it right, your efforts will be appreciated and understood by most listeners.

TIP:

Did you realize that there are many different degrees of agreement and disagreement? Did you know that when most of us say "yes" or "no" to a question, we are being imprecise? We just say these words because they are short and easy, but much of the time we don't really intend to use them with the full power of their meaning. This is because "yes" or "no" are absolutes. "Yes" means "yes, completely and without reservation, limitation, or condition," unless you express a reservation, limitation, or condition. No is the same in its absoluteness. To communicate precisely, you should be sensitive to this distinction.

Over the next few days, practice listening very carefully to – and answering carefully and precisely – all the informal yes/no forced-choice questions that fly around you during your day. You may find it very enlightening. Being more sensitive to this unique communications issue will make you a better, more truthful communicator.

Ex.: "Are you ready to go to work?" (The old answer to this one was "yes.") The precise answer, which is conditional and limited, might be something like this: "If you are asking if I am prepared to depart, the answer is "yes." If you are asking if I feel ready for work, that answer is "no."

Ex.: "Do I look good in this dress?" (The old answer was "Yes, Darling.") The precise answer, which is conditional and limited, might be something like this: " Yes, I like how you look, but it is not about the dress. Specifically, I like how happy you are with that dress, since you love it. I like how you look when you are happy. However, I don't know anything about fashion or about dresses – so I have no idea how to actually evaluate the dress." (Okay – this one might get sticky…)

The point is, for the purpose of testimony, you want to practice telling the precise form (rather than the imprecise or "social form") of the truth whenever you can.

Other Common Obstacles

Inaccurate or Unacceptable Words and Phrases

You are likely to encounter questions containing words or phrases that you simply would never use to name or characterize people and/or events in the case. If these words or phrases don't quite sound right, if they don't precisely capture the truth as you see it, you should not agree to use them merely because the questioner has inserted them into the question. Look at these examples:

Q. "Mr. Jones, you were driving your brother's souped-up sports coupe that evening, weren't you?"

If you are Mr. Jones, and you know that your brother's car is a high-performance car, but don't think it's quite accurate to term it a "souped-up sports coupe," you may wish to reject the characterization. You have the right to do this, of course, as "not quite accurate" is the same as "not true"!

If you agree to answer a question that contains inaccurate terms, you are — as said earlier — tacitly agreeing that those terms express the truth. You should try to guard against this. On some topics, it may not be "a big deal," but there may also be instances where the characterization of the car you are driving (for example) is, for listeners, a statement about the kind of person you are.

You will not know how any of these small inaccuracies might shape the perceptions of listeners, so you should not ignore them or let them go. Bring them up with the questioner anytime they appear, even if they seem minor. Gatekeeping takes discipline and perseverance.

You may wonder how to do this politely and appropriately, as you will not want to create the wrong impression. You should never quibble or debate or play word games with a questioner. That is not a good idea at all, as most listeners will not like it. But you still must deal with the use of an inaccurate or incorrect term.

Since characterizing the car in our example might be important, you will probably have thought about it before this interview. You will have decided the most accurate way to describe the car—the truth about that car. You will thus be prepared for this type of question. Then the goal is to remember to handle it politely.

Speak courteously. It matters. The man or woman in the hotseat should always be the nicest person in the room. Others might argue or swagger, some listener might be irritable, and someone else might not be paying attention. However, you will be on your best behavior so that nothing about the way you act interferes with people's ability to listen to and consider the truth you are there to tell.

TIP:

Most of us do not have a great deal of experience politely and carefully filtering and correcting inaccuracies in the communications of others in a formal environment like that of a public hearing or a courtroom. The good news is that it is not hard to learn!

Here are some styles of courteous answers using the question above about the "souped-up sports coupe." Note that all contain a rejection of an inaccurate term. Most contain a rejection and one other thing.

Q. "Mr. Jones, you were driving your brother's souped-up sports coupe that evening, weren't you?"

Style of Answer: (simple rejection) "I wouldn't agree that his car is "souped-up."

Style of Answer: (apologize; then reject) "I'm sorry. I wouldn't use the term "souped-up sports coupe."

Style of Answer: (agree with the true part of the question, then reject) "It is a sports coupe, but "souped up" isn't what I'd call it."

Style of Answer: (reject, then correct) "I wouldn't call it "souped-up," but it certainly is a high-quality performance car."

Try this out in casual conversations with friends! When you listen carefully, you will be surprised at how many half-correct/half-incorrect statements are made to you over the course of a day. Gently, politely, thoughtfully reject and – if possible – correct! Your friends may be surprised when you first do this, so explain to them what you are doing and why.

Confusing Questions

Confusing or awkwardly phrased questions are often easy to misunderstand. The problem isn't yours alone, as listeners will also have difficulty tracking with a poorly worded question. The correct thing for you to do if you find that the question is awkward or that it just sounds "weird" to you is ask to have it reworded. Simply tell the questioner the truth; that the question is hard to follow, or sounds funny to you. Tell him you aren't sure that you understand it, and request that he try again. Both the questioner and your attorney know that you have the right to ask this.

You may be asked to identify the aspect of the question causing you problems. If you can answer that, you should try to do so. However, even if you can't explain exactly why a question doesn't make sense (and you may not be able to—after all, it doesn't make sense to begin with), you shouldn't try to answer until the question is asked in a way that makes sense to you. As noted earlier in this handbook, you should assert the right to be asked an answerable question; that means a question you understand.

Think about this: How can you answer a question with honesty if you honestly don't know what the question really means?

Confusion is Not YOUR Problem

Many witnesses feel uncomfortable when a question leaves them confused. Don't let that happen to you. You should know that a confusing question is the lawyer's responsibility; his problem, not yours. All you are required to do is answer questions. If the question is not answerable because it is confusing to you, the lawyer will have to do something with it. He'll need to restate it or go on to something else.

He may challenge you by asking it again in exactly the same words, suggesting that you are avoiding the question. Stick to your guns! If it was confusing the first time it was asked, it probably will still be confusing the second time. So, tell him again that it is confusing. Then, just sit there and wait for him to fix it. Sit quietly and wait.

You should not play games with the attorney asking you questions. So, do not claim a question is confusing if it is not. But, occasionally one that seems as though it should be no problem to answer will still trigger a feeling of alarm. The question itself isn't confusing, but it has a confusing effect. Sometimes a very straightforward-sounding question nevertheless gets your brain spinning and you start to feel disoriented, as though you are being pulled away from the truth. If that happens to you, tell him so. That is the truth. It could be that he is intentionally trying to create that effect.

Attorneys are often taught to ask questions in patterns. A common pattern might be called "One, two, three. Bam!" This pattern involves being asked to agree with three (or two, or five – but three is the most common) simple, very logical sounding assertions one after another, then being challenged by a final assertion which sounds irrefutable given that you've agreed with the ones that went before. But, notice I said that it only sounds irrefutable. But, you may not feel it to be true, even though you can't explain why. That's what could be making you feel so uncomfortable.

If this happens to you, you should feel okay about saying that, while the concluding idea may sound reasonable, there is something about it that is creating confusion for you. You should testify that it sounds right, but you are not sure that it really is right. That is the whole truth. It sounds right, but you are not sure if it actually is. Then, just sit there. Silent.

Silence is Your Friend

A key skill in gatekeeping of the truth is to be able to be silent, especially if you've just rejected what seems to be a logical conclusion. You may find yourself wanting to fill the gap when a lawyer is working on a question or riffling through documents. He might even just sit there and stare at you! If that happens, you could feel a very strong urge to fill the gap and just give him something, anything. You may want to comment or to offer some information related to the general topic being asked about at the time. This is very natural in ordinary conversation. However, don't do it here. Let the silence rule the moment. Clear your mind. Wait for a re-formulated question or a new question. Let it be his problem to solve, as it should be. This is the best policy.

When you are silent after such an exchange, you are also giving yourself time to get rid of any interference in your mind. Sometimes interference will manifest itself as a little voice in the back of your head. Your inner voice might be asking worried-sounding questions: "What happened just now?"

"Why does it sound true and feel not true at the same time?" "Am I getting something mixed up?" "Oh, my gosh! I feel so dumb!" My advice is that you just take a moment to let that voice quiet down.

You should not be trying to answer the worrying questioner in the back of your mind. The real questioner is sitting across the table. You don't need two examiners! So, simply let yourself set aside those worrying thoughts and attend to the moment at hand. Just try to relax and breathe. Have a drink of water, or ask if you might stand up and stretch. Do something to break the tension. Chances are that you will realize later what it was that confused you. But, don't worry about it now.

Be patient with yourself and try to do the job you are there to do. Stick to your oath. Tell the truth, even if the truth is that you are confused by a question and don't know why.

Correcting Mistakes

You may realize at some point in your testimony that you got something wrong at an earlier point in the questioning. You may have said Bill was in a meeting when it was actually Bob, or that you took a course in "management" when it was actually called a course in "supervision". You might have gotten a date wrong, or agreed to a proposition that you now realize to be erroneous. Take this advice: Correct your testimony as soon as you realize you have made a mistake.

The interference from having made a misstatement or error can be very strong. The voice in the back of your mind can really get itself going on this: "Oh, my gosh! I've just committed perjury!"

"I'm an idiot!" "I've just lost all of my credibility!" "Who will believe anything I say now?" It can be very uncomfortable.

The energy drain from this dilemma should be halted right away. Take heart. You did not commit perjury. All you did was make a mistake. You are not an idiot, either; you are just in the hotseat and the hotseat can be tough. Importantly, you will not lose credibility if you stop the action and correct your mistake. Actually, the effect will be the opposite. Just do it.

Here's an example:

Q: "Now, Mr. Jones, I want to ask you a question about some emails that you wrote. Let me show you some printouts and ask you if you recognize them."

A: "I'm sorry. Before we cover this, I need to make a correction. I just realized that a few minutes ago I answered one of your questions wrongly when I said that I attended the safety meeting at headquarters in March of 2012. I remember now that I missed that meeting because I was ill that day."

The correction can occur at any time. It doesn't have to be relevant to the question at hand. It doesn't have to be smooth or eloquent. And, if it's embarrassing to you, you might consider saying that, too, and getting it off your chest. The important thing is to get it done and remove the interference.

Hypothetical Questions:

Talk to someone who understands legal testimony and get him or her to tell you about hypothetical or "what if" questions. These questions are usually a trap because you cannot stick tightly to the truth with a hypothetical question.

Hypothetical questions are difficult because the "what if" events aren't actually happening and haven't actually happened. In the strictest sense, you can't answer truthfully about any questions based upon assumptions. Your answer would not actually be truth. Your answer would be at best an honest guess based on one or more assumptions. If a questioner wants you to work from assumptions, he or she is intentionally or unintentionally creating a trap for you. Don't get caught in it.

You should consider speaking to the fundamental truth about any "what if" question the first time you are asked one. You should remind the questioner up front that any answer you give would be just a guess, however sincere, and you can't know if it would be right. That's the truth about hypothetical questions.

Some professionals (physicians, scientists, and engineers, for example) testify under oath frequently in cases in which their knowledge may be helpful. They are usually called "expert witnesses" and have been trained to analyze hypothetical scenarios. They are often asked to do just that for the purposes of giving legal testimony. They may frequently be obliged to answer this unique type of question.

They know how to filter assumptions and how to form and scientifically limit the conclusions that emerge from "what-if" thinking. They almost always attach appropriate limiting statements to their opinions, reminding the questioner and the audience that they are basically guessing, even if from a highly informed perspective. Proceeding extremely carefully and being tentative in answering hypothetical questions is not some form of evasion or avoidance. It is intellectual honesty.

TIP:

As general preparation for hypothetical "what-if" questions, think about this idea: When you are asked such a what-if question, you are limited to the assumptions the questioner gives you in the question. There may be other assumptions you would have included if you had thought of the scenario yourself or that you will think of later. The question occurs in a kind of vacuum. Therefore, you should limit your answer with very specific language that communicates the truth, both about your answer and the reality that you might think of it differently at another time. Your limiting remarks usually should be made before you answer the question. They might sound like this:

Q. "I want to ask a what-if question. If you had a two-ton widget and a 1.5 ton truck and your driver was Italian and it was raining, you would never load that widget onto that truck, would you?"

A. One way to do it is start with the eternal truth about hypotheticals:

"This is a what-if question. My answer will be a guess. With that said, I might not load that widget on that truck."

B. Another way is to limit your answer with the truth about this particular what-if question:

"Right here, right now, as you give me those assumptions to work with, I might be worried whether the European driver was good at converting kilograms to tons."

Background Facts Missing in Question

Unfortunately, you are sooner or later likely to find yourself in the hotseat being asked questions in which the background facts (perhaps known to you and to the questioner) are probably not known to the listener. As pointed out earlier, this can lead to a misunderstanding of the true meaning of both the question and the answer. If you are asked a question you can't answer fully without giving background information, you should say so immediately. This is good gatekeeping. You are preventing any misunderstanding of your testimony.

The test is simple. If you think your answer will be misunderstood or lead to an incorrect conclusion about the truth by an uninformed listener who doesn't know the necessary history, you essentially have a duty to point that out in order to prevent such misunderstanding. If you are testifying in court, you will have taken an oath to provide testimony that is the truth, the whole truth, and nothing but the truth. Putting the needed background information into your answer meets the requirement of your oath.

You should assume this "testimony" stance in any hotseat setting. Answering a question without the needed background is to fall short of your duty. You are the judge of whether some history is needed to make a complete answer. No one else decides it.

Do not misunderstand this advice as an invitation to make frequent long and complicated answers, as they will sound like excuses and guilty explanations for what you may have done or not done. Complicated answers may also seem evasive, and listeners will be impatient with you.

You should continue to follow the earlier advice to make short and simple answers whenever possible. However, there will also be many legitimate instances in which you have to give historical background in order for an answer to make sense.

TIP:

Knowing how to politely and appropriately manage situations in which you need to include background in an answer to accurately testify is helpful.

Below are some examples of different ways such questions might be handled. Remember always to give the answer first. Don't start with the background, as it may sound as though you are trying to avoid the question.

Q. "Ms. Jones, isn't it true that you never read the manual for the Model 3-B instrument panel before installing it?"

Answer: (State the truthful answer, and then state that there is background – a "reason.")

A. "That's true, and there is a reason for that."

Answer: (State the truthful answer, and press for a follow up question.)

A. "That's true, and there is some history the people here should know concerning that issue."

Answer: (State the truthful answer and attach at least part of the history to it.)

A. "That's true, and there's an interesting history that relates to the Model 3-C manual and how we came to use that newer document."

Inaccurate or Incomplete Context in Questions

Accurate context, as mentioned earlier in this handbook, is often the key to understanding the meaning of both the question and the answer. By the time you get to the hotseat, you should have thought about whether you might need context explanations, often in the form of background stories, in order to speak to the whole truth with regard to a particular issue.

Having done that homework, and having considered how to put key topics in their correct context and in the clearest fashion, you will have a more sensitive ear for any questions that get it wrong. Then you will be ready assert the need for the context — and deliver it.

You will also need to apply the rules of politeness and courtesy we have discussed.

TIP:

Try this in your preparation for an interview. Request a friend or colleague (a friend who is an attorney would be best!) to ask you some questions (on any topic) of the form used in legal cross-examination. Have him try to create questions that need some correction or elaboration of context in order to be fully answered and understood. Then practice the reject-and-correct exercise on each question. The questions don't even have to be about the topic at hand. In fact, it is better if they are not. What matters is that you learn to listen for questions that need a contextualized answer and then handle them honestly and politely. Remember, we are dealing with necessary explanations only, not excuses or evasions. The task here is to get the truth out for the listener.

Example: Q. "Mr. Jones, the training for your job as safety manager seems to have involved only a single one-week course — is that correct?"

Example Answer: (reject only)

"A. I don't think that's correct."

Example Answer: (apologize; reject and correct with an accurately stated fact)

A. "I'm sorry, I don't think that describes my training at all; though I did take a safety related classroom course."

Example Answer: (reject and deconstruct the question, addressing some essential element of it)

A. "No, a safety manager's training requires a lot more than that."

Example Answer: (reject and reconstruct the proposition completely)

A. "Actually, the training for my job as safety manager included ten years working as a safety inspector and supervisor in several different areas, as well as a one-week course on applying OSHA regulations."

You will most likely have to clarify the context of critical issues raised in some of the questions you are asked. You will also want listeners to trust you when you take the time to explain something to them. They will trust you if you do this only when it is absolutely necessary in order for them to have the complete picture, and if you explain in clear language and in short statements.

When you do these things; adhere vigorously to the truth, use precise language, refer to background facts, keep the context and story in mind, detect out-of-context questions, reject and correct inaccuracy, and maintain politeness and courtesy at all times, you will succeed at defending your truth.

More About Gatekeeping

It's Not Necessarily Wrong to Have Notes

Sometimes a witness is obliged to testify with regard to a long or complex series of events. The order in which those events occurred may be relevant to the issues at hand in the case. Unfortunately, there might be a lot of them and it can be hard to keep track of which event happened when! If you find yourself preparing to be in this type of testifying situation and are worried that you might get things mixed up and out of order, consider asking your lawyer to help you prepare a timeline of the key events. You can use the timeline during your testimony as notes to help you keep the dates straight. The rules of evidence require that this timeline be shown to the opposing attorney, but it could be that it alleviates so much stress for you that it is still a good idea to do it.

This principle, that notes are not necessarily a bad thing for a witness, extends itself to other types of written material that help you keep track of details. It might be a list of the names of people or an equipment inventory or the places on a map. This is merely data, not some kind of cheat-sheet for testifying. It should be thought of as what it is, a helpful tool so that a witness can keep the record straight.

Testifying about Memories

Witnesses are often obliged to testify in cases that concern something that happened years before. A common problem here is the witness' uncertainty about some of his memories. Sometimes witnesses think memories aren't valid testimony because they can't remember all the details. You need not make this mistake.

It is very natural for people to only remember an event in "pieces", a patchwork of images, or a clear memory of only a few moments. We tend to store little video clips in our brain, much like the videos many people store on a phone or electronic tablet. Sometimes these images are disjointed and hard to place. They are fragmented. But, they are still evidence. They are still the truth. As the gate-keeper of the truth, you should be ready to protect the integrity of these fragments of evidence.

You can learn to testify to the truth about your fragments of memory using precise language that explains what you remember and what you don't. If you vividly remember seeing an accident, but don't' remember where you were standing or what you were doing there, then, that is the truth. You should tell the questioner that you have a partial memory, but that you are confident about what you do remember. Not being able to remember all the details shouldn't weaken your confidence. That is the point.

The other side of the memory coin is that there are almost certainly things you would remember clearly if they had actually happened. If a pink elephant sat on your mother when you were five years old, you would never forget it! Likewise, if your co-worker threatened another co-worker with a gun, you would not forget that either. You can testify confidently about such things. The honest testimony on certain issues is that if such-and-such had actually happened, you absolutely would remember it! Your sincere confidence in the negative can be a powerful truth. Ex.: "I'm sorry. I'm confident my boss didn't insult anybody that day. That would be so out of character for him that it would have registered with me strongly – and I would remember it."

Point in Time

Another important part of gatekeeping is to be very clear about the time reference of a question. For example, a witness may be asked a about what he knows with regard to a certain event. But, there is a problem. The witness knows things about it now, at the time of questioning, but didn't know about those things then, when the event happened, nor for long after it happened. Witnesses sometimes get confused about how to handle these questions.

You should always make sure that you know the time reference of a question. If you are asked to discuss your view on a topic, it could very well be that you hold a different view now than you held a year ago. If that is the case, ask the questioner if he wants to know what you thought then or what you think now. Alternatively, you might answer by giving him both views and explaining that your opinion changed and what changed it. In either event, you are fulfilling your obligation to testify to the whole truth. In so doing, you are also making it easier for the judge and/or jury to understand your testimony.

Here's an example: Q: "You know it's a violation of OSHA standards for a company to fail to provide safety gloves for handling those chemicals, don't you?"

A: "I certainly know that now, but I actually didn't know it two years ago, when we had that chemical spill."

Q: "Are you trying to make it okay to violate safety standards just because you don't know about them?"

A: "Of course not. I am just trying to be clear about what I knew and when I knew it."

Implication

When something is suggested in a question, but not said directly, we say that it has been "implied", or that an "implication" has been made. You will likely encounter some questioning where the attorney is trying to make a point by implication. If you think that your testimony is being used to support an implication that is not true, you should feel free to say so as part of your answer. To fail to do so would be to fall short as a gatekeeper of the whole truth. Commenting on a false implication is the responsible thing to do.

Let's look at an example:

Q: "People shouldn't do things that are illegal, wouldn't you agree?

A: "I would generally agree with that, sure."

Q: "And if an organization was doing something illegal, that would be wrong, wouldn't it?"

A: "I think that usually doing illegal stuff is wrong, yes."

Q: "And if a company is doing illegal stuff, they should be punished for it, shouldn't they?"

A: "I'm sorry. The implication in these questions seems to be that my company was doing something illegal, and I don't think that's true."

You probably noticed in the example above that the implication was being built through the use of a pattern of questions. The witness waited for the implication to become clear before pointing out the problem. That is the right way for you to do it, too.

The witness promptly agreed with the obvious, people usually shouldn't do illegal things. Then he agreed with another obvious thing, organizations shouldn't do illegal things either. But, as he felt the implication becoming clear, he then pointed out the truth. The questioner was implying that the witness should agree that his company needed to be punished. Since the witness didn't believe that to be true, he pointed out the incorrect implication. He was gatekeeping, protecting the whole truth.

A good questioner would probably push back on the witness, saying that wasn't what was asked, and there might be some further wrangling over the issue. But, the point has been made, the truth guarded.

De-stabilizing Questions

It is not at all uncommon for witnesses to encounter questions, usually early in a deposition or at the beginning of cross-examination, that don't seem to have been asked for any great reason other than to make the witness uncomfortable. The effect of questions that are embarrassing to answer or which are confusing by their unexpectedness is to create interference in the witness' mind. The witness starts worrying about his credibility. He may even begin to doubt himself. That inner voice starts its worrying chatter, and the real substantive stuff of the testimony hasn't even been raised yet! You will want to be ready for this.

Let's look at a couple of examples of de-stabilizing questions:

Q: "You spent a lot of time preparing for this testimony today, didn't you?"

A: "I don't know what you mean by a lot of time, but I did spend about two days preparing with my attorney."

Q: "You are saying that you needed two entire days with a lawyer just to come here and tell the truth?"

A: "I certainly did spend two days preparing. And of course I am here to testify to the truth!"

Notice how relaxed the above witness sounds? The common questioning pattern used by the attorney here is designed to get witnesses worried about the propriety of having spent a considerable amount of time in preparation for their testimony. The questioning attorney wants the witness to think that taking a lot of time to prepare will look bad to a judge or jury. He wants to make the witness worry that having spent several days with an attorney will make him appear to have been coached to give some kind of made-up testimony. If you get asked this type of question, you should stay just as relaxed as the witness in the above example.

The truth is that witnesses sometimes need weeks of preparation for testimony that is technically complex or highly detailed. Think about that: Not days. Weeks!

Every lawyer in the room (and the judge, too, if these questions are asked at trial!) knows that taking two days or more for your preparation is absolutely reasonable. They will know that he is just asking the question to try to get you de-stabilized, to create interference that might reduce your readiness for the more serious questioning to come. Now you know it, too. Don't fear such questions. You were helped by an attorney to prepare to testify to the truth with clarity and precision and you were taught how to manage the questioning process. That is a good thing.

How about another example:

Q: "You're being paid to come here and testify for your company, aren't you?"

A: "I wouldn't say that I am being paid to testify for the company. What is correct is that I am being compensated by the company for my time. I am here to testify to the truth."

Notice how this witness stays relaxed, too. The questioning pattern is an old stand-by for attorneys trying to embarrass a witness. This witness knows the difference between being paid for his time and being paid to say what the company might want him to say. He knows that he is there to testify to the truth. The company may want him to testify because they believe that the truth he brings helps to support their view of the case, but that is different. That is not a compromise of his integrity or a violation of his oath as a witness. You can and should mark out this line confidently, too. Testifying in behalf or a company while being paid as an employee or consultant for that company can be something you are proud of and pleased to do when you remember do it this way.

Being a Spokesperson

If you are reading this book because you think at some point you may be called to serve as a witness in a legal proceeding, but think it unlikely that you would ever be a spokesperson, take my advice and read the following section anyway. There is much to be gained by thinking about the unique role of the spokesperson. The spokesperson, you see, must answer questions not just for himself, but in behalf of others as well.

Some of the pressures faced by spokespersons, such as being asked questions in the context of a tragedy or answering questions in a hostile public atmosphere, are also sometimes faced by witnesses in legal settings. There is much to learn.

There is actually a unique testifying scenario in civil lawsuits involving companies and other organizations. Frequently, a person is designated as the corporate representative of a company or organization and must testify as though his answers are the answers of the company. If you are a manager or executive, there is at least some chance that you may one day find yourself in exactly that role. It can be quite challenging, but you can learn to negotiate this territory by relying upon many of the same tools you have been learning with regard to being a witness. Let's examine a few interesting aspects of being a spokesperson.

Tragedy and Crisis: The Toughest Context

A particularly difficult hotseat is that occupied by a spokesperson for a company after a tragedy has occurred. A terrible accident may earn you some unwanted time in the spotlight. You will need to prepare for this as well as you can, even if there is not always a great deal of time. It is essential that you have some support and assistance in this preparation because it is sometimes hard to get focused on answering questions during a difficult time. It still needs to be done and done right. That means spending time in preparation.

In the best of worlds you would have a trained public relations person in this role, but sometimes such resources are not available. Frequently, even if you work in a setting where public relations people are doing much of the addressing of these issues with the media, you will still have to answer questions. It could be that you have to answer to a board or commission, to clients, customers, or shareholders, or to attorneys.

Remember What Matters

Always remember in immediate post-tragedy communications that human suffering is the most important matter. It is the defining context for the conversation and should remain so throughout. It should be the first thing on your mind and the first thing you speak about. Consider this advice: no matter what question comes first in an immediate post-event interview, the first answer should always be an acknowledgment of the tragedy of the event and of the pain and loss of those involved.

Being a spokesperson is all about the truth, and the truth is that human costs are the ones that count.

Acknowledge in your first response the two truths that often go unspoken after a tragedy: the event is heartbreaking to all, and you and the people in your organization are as saddened by it as anyone. Do not fail to say this, obvious as it sounds. The reality is that you will more than likely be experiencing feelings of compassion and sorrow. You should speak to this truth immediately and directly. Failing to deliver the words aloud and with sincerity can create steep subsequent costs to your credibility.

Another thing point may seem obvious: you should think about how to speak to the event and your reaction to it with the same care and commitment to truthfulness and accuracy that you would apply to delivering testimony in a courtroom. The words you select and the characterizations you utilize may place a permanent imprint on the moment. This is a time for thoughtfulness.

The exchange might sound like this:

Q. "Thanks for being here, Ms. Jones. Can you give us a quick rundown on what your company is doing in response to this tragic explosion at your plant?"

A. "Before I answer that, I want to say that what matters most is the terrible loss to the Ross family. Everybody at Acme is deeply saddened by this event. We lost a good friend and long-time employee and can only imagine how heartbreaking it must be for his family. Our thoughts and prayers are with them.

Now, let me tell you where we are in our response to this tragedy."

Don't Try to Explain

If an event has only just occurred, and you are making a first contact with the media, do not be tempted to somehow explain what happened. Even if you are quite sure you understand the cause and origin of an accident, you should refrain from finalizing a conclusion. Why? Because, confident or not, you would be speculating! You will not have done a thorough investigation yet. You will have not let the coolness of time foster the objectivity required for such work. This is the mirror opposite of adding context to make an answer complete. In an instance like this, the context (the findings from an investigation) is not yet established. That is the complete truth.

Too many accidents get "explained" wrongly in the excitement of early news conferences. Victims often have been wrongly blamed for causing their own injury. Likewise, fingers have been speculatively pointed at companies and products. Third party "culprits" have been unfairly identified and stigmatized. In many instances, this happens when spokespersons speculate or attempt to answer speculative questions. For your part, you should keep yourself from forming an early attachment to some theory of the cause of the event. That will help you keep yourself honest in any interviews. Think *testimony*.

About "No Comment"

Before you make a mistake in the opposite direction, let's make sure that you never let the words "no comment" cross your lips. Few responses can draw more ire than this one. So, you ask, how should I handle questions that I am just not ready to answer? The answer is that you should stand on the rock of truth well-spoken. The precise truth is almost certainly not that you have no comment. The precise truth is that it is too early to comment. It would be guessing. It would be reckless. It would be unfair. A clear and truthful handling of such a situation should sound something like this:

Q. "Mr. Jones! Mr. Jones! What comment do you have on the charge that your safety plan was inadequate at this plant?"

A. "We can't answer the charge because the event hasn't been investigated yet. I'm anticipating we will take a hard look at all aspects of safety. Everybody at Acme wants to prevent such tragedies as this one."

Be Responsible

If you are going to the hotseat as spokesperson for a company, remember that taking responsibility and acting responsibly is not the same as "admitting responsibility (i.e., legal fault). Initiating a purposeful plan of response is not somehow an admission of liability on the part of your company. Many people get this absolutely wrong, bury their heads in the sand, and try to go on with business as usual. The result is that, out of fear of appearing guilty, the company operates as though the event didn't happen.

Doing nothing traps everyone in a kind of disingenuous stance because the truth is that something did happen, and people at the company do want to respond. This wish to respond is not caused by guilt. It is urged, rather, by compassion.

You can responsibly express the shock and grief your people are feeling. You can express a wish to provide aid and comfort, if possible. You can express a desire to understand what happened. You can express determination to prevent further harm.

This is the responsible approach of honest and compassionate adults and is expected by other adults. Armed with the ability to speak to this aspect of truth, you will be much better able to address the media, agency investigators, and—inevitably—attorneys.

Part of succeeding in the hotseat is feeling free to be normal. That means to have normal compassion, to want to do normal things to help others, to have normal questions, even normal self-doubt with regard to whether or not you could have done something more, something that might have prevented a tragedy. In a post-tragedy interview, the best way for you to be in the right frame of mind to represent your organization effectively is for you to feel confident that you are doing everything you can.

Introduce Your Answer, Then Answer

As discussed earlier, you should learn to introduce answers to questions by prefacing them with the key contextual realities. By tagging your answers with the truth about why they matter, you remind everyone, including yourself, where the focus should be. Think about this example:

You are the spokesperson for Acme Corp. There was an accidental explosion at the plant yesterday, and Mr. Ross died in the aftermath. His family is grief-stricken, shocked. Everyone at the plant is upset; employees are weeping over the loss of a friend. Your company is offering to help the family with any immediate needs. Your company president has called the widow to extend his condolences. You are putting together an accident investigation team. Correctly, there are police and agency investigators already looking at the event.

Q. "Ms. Jones, is there any truth to the rumor that there are already federal investigators in your plant, looking at how this accident happened?"

A. "This was a terrible and heartbreaking accident. We want to know how it came to occur. We welcome the assistance of various authorities, including local, state, and federal investigators because that will help us understand what happened."

This answer reminds the listener (and the speaker reminds herself) about the context. It sends home the message of the truth: the people at the company are hurting, too. The people at the company don't yet have the answers about how the accident happened. In that context, of course, they are cooperating with government investigators.

Subsequent questions should draw additional context reminders.

Q. "Ms. Jones, how do you answer the charges of the ex-employee who says this accident was just waiting to happen?"

A. "Right now, Mr. Ross's family is really having a hard time. Our management and employees are grieving, too. I don't know how to answer those charges at this time. I'm sure we will learn more very soon."

Notice how Ms. Jones doesn't get defensive. She sticks with what is important. A very sad thing has happened, and a man has died. His family is in grief, as are the people at the company. She can't answer the specific question, and she says so. But, importantly, she did have a response. She answered with context alone. That is an important thing to understand. Sometimes the context is itself the only answer that matters. It's about trying to speak to the essential truth.

Common "Problem" Questions

A number of common kinds of questions must be dealt with gracefully and smoothly by spokespersons. Some of these will appear quite frequently in your interviews. These questions may make you uncomfortable, but only if you don't know how to handle them.

Generally, there are two large categories of problem questions. The first is one in which the problem is explicit in the wording of the question itself, the dilemma obvious. The second type is a question in which the problem is implicit. It is tonal or thematic rather than directly stated. These are a little harder to recognize, but you can learn to tune your "radar" to detect them. Then you can learn to deal with them.

Here are examples of each:

Explicit: "Mr. Jones, can you tell us all the things your organization is doing to manage this emergency?"

Let's assume there actually is an "emergency." Here's a question where an absolute quantity has been explicitly requested, i.e., "all the things." You can rarely give an absolute answer that is the absolute truth. So don't try. Limit your answer and take the "all-ness" out.

Perhaps an answer might sound like this:

Answer: "I'm not sure I can give you an exhaustive list, but I can point out several of the things we are working on right now."

Now let's look at a statement with the other type of problem, an implied judgment by the questioner.

Implicit: "Mr. Jones, we know your organization has just those three teams moving into place to work on this emergency. Where are you turning for additional resources?"

There's more than one implicit conclusion here, isn't there? The questioner seems to be pre-supposing that "those three teams" aren't enough. He also seems to be thinking that you will need outside help to get the job done.

How to keep on the path of accuracy and truth? You probably should handle both these implicit issues in an introduction to your response, and then go right into an answer to the question about "additional resources." This strategy would work best for a press conference or other setting in which questioners are taking turns. Answering it all as one piece gives the questioner (and listeners) a complete answer.

It might sound like this:

Q: "Mr. Jones, we know your organization has just those three teams moving into place to work on this emergency. Where are you turning for additional resources?"

A: "This is a complex and evolving situation. Right now, we think we are going at it correctly with our three-team approach. As things develop, we may very well add more resources to the effort."

Notice how Mr. Jones correctly reminds the listener that this is a dynamic and fluid scenario. Then he signals confidence in what the company is doing right now while correctly being open to the idea that the company might need to bring in more help at some point.

Alternatively, a spokesperson might reject and correct, which is done with an answer that gently rejects the implication and awaits a follow-up question. Such an approach works better in a one-on-

one interview or when speaking to a board, where the original questioner gets to do the follow-up.

It might sound like this:

Q: "Mr. Jones, we know your organization has just those three teams moving into place to work on this emergency. Where are you turning for additional resources?"

A: "We are confident that our three teams are working all the key problems right now."

Mr. Jones corrects the implication that three teams aren't enough ("right now") and waits for the questioner to follow-up.

Let's look at some more types of challenging questions you might encounter in a press conference or at a public meeting:

Hostile or Insulting Tone

Sometimes questions are asked in a way that is simply offensive. The words themselves might not be a problem if you were to read them in an e-mail, for example. Unfortunately, you could be stuck at a podium with a camera pointed at you while you confront a sneering expression and a sarcastically-toned question. The actual subject of the question might be simple, easy to handle. Yet the question still upsets you because of the delivery. What should you do?

First, never meet perceived hostility with hostility of your own. If the questioner really is on the offensive, he may have an entire arsenal of attack topics. Don't return the fire. Since he may be well prepared, and you have no idea what else he may come up with, the odds are that you will lose in the ensuing exchange. Unfortunately, it is also likely that you will simply come out looking and sounding defensive. Worse, you may be seen as arrogant or disrespectful of others.

You should remember that the question may not have sounded particularly offensive to other listeners who are present. You should also consider the possibility that you are getting it wrong, that no offense is intended, that your eye or ear is tricking you. Take this advice: answer that question in a straight-up manner, and be as rigorously truthful as you can be, as though the hostile tone weren't there. Put your kindest and most agreeable self into the answer. Then wait to see what happens next.

If a questioner truly is hostile or is trying to use a hostile tone to provoke you, he must decide whether to drop the attack in the light of your serene response or carry on with it. If he carries on, chances are that he will be more direct and aggressive in the next question. What to do now?

Generally, you should try to handle the second one the same way you handled the first. Make a truthful, agreeably delivered response as though there had been no sarcasm and no sneering in the question. You have now let him know you are not going to be easily provoked.

If he does it a third time, he will almost surely put a harder edge in either the words or the tone, probably both. Now you can respond. You have gained the right to do it. Your politeness purchases a kind of moral currency that can be exchanged for certain privileges, including the right to openly rebuke an insult. But don't do it—not yet. You may not have to spend all that you have earned.

It is often better to draw out an attack even further. This can be done in several ways, some of them touched upon in earlier sections of this book. They include

Politely question the question:

"I'm sorry. I'm not sure I understand the question. Can you ask it a different way?"

Politely ask the questioner for help:

"I'm sorry, I'm not sure I understand the question. What would you like me to address?"

Politely confess your confusion:

"I'm sorry, I'm not sure I understand the question. Is there something obvious that I am missing?"

I want to remind you that you are not here to play games with a questioner. Don't let yourself seek to "win" the exchange. The above techniques have the purpose of dissipating his (and perhaps your) aggressive energy. However, the goal remains the same, getting the truth told clearly and well.

Keep drawing it out, and at some point you will get a question that you can answer with the simplicity and accuracy you intend, and which won't be part of a point-counter-point argument. That's what you want: to answer questions clearly and straightforwardly, not debate the questioner. Truth that is told as argument often gets lost in the heat and smoke. Quieter is better.

Often, as in public hearings, some questioners don't actually want answers. They just want to vent their feelings. You may not have to ever answer some of these types of questions. Remember to give questioners the benefit of the doubt: they may truly believe that you or your organization has done something wrong. They may be legitimately aggrieved persons who need a forum. They may be victims or the families of victims. If they just need to say it, often the best thing to do is to politely and respectfully stand there and let them say it.

If you operate from a posture of respect for any and all questioners and questions, you will fare much better.

One of the most important rules of thumb: Breathe. Just take your time and remember to breathe. Hostile exchanges often move fast, they accelerate as the anger escalates. A deliberately slowly paced and polite response almost always suppresses the angry attack. And, importantly, you will have retained the moral currency discussed earlier. If you absolutely have to confront a persistently hostile or irritating questioner, you will have the standing you need to do so. You will have been polite and patient and sincere. But sometimes you will actually have to deal with it a bit more directly.

How to Stop a Hostile Questioner in a Public Setting

Politely apologize and ask him to take a break:

"I'm sorry. I have been trying very hard to answer your questions. But I think we have gotten as far as we can get for now. Perhaps later we can address your issues further?"

Politely apologize and state an intent to change topics for the good of the other attendees:

"I'm sorry. I have been trying very hard to answer all your questions on this topic. But I think there are other things to cover and other people with questions that I should try to accommodate."

Politely apologize and turn him over to the group:

"I'm sorry. I have been trying very hard to answer all your questions on this topic. Perhaps there are others here who have information or ideas that would be helpful to you and with whom you can speak later."

Politely apologize and refuse to address him further:

"I'm sorry, but I have tried very hard to answer all of your questions on this topic. I'm not going to answer any more. Thank you."

You can use more than one of the above techniques, of course. Sometimes it takes several splashes of cool water to put out the fire.

Why Did You Do X? and/or Why Didn't You Do X?

Sometimes you will be asked questions that presuppose your actions (or those of your company or organization) to be wrong or insufficient. Alternatively, you may be asked questions that seem to posit that another set of actions is superior to the ones you have chosen.

Usually you will have thought about and prepared yourself to explain your actions and will know the answer to such questions. You will have considered alternate courses and will be able to discuss why one path was chosen over another. But occasionally you will get asked about something for which you haven't prepared yourself. What to do?

First, as always, be honest. In a situation of this type, before you make any attempt at an answer, you should just tell the questioner that prior to the question you haven't considered things in the way asked. Such a confession of vulnerability typically earns you a right to some amount of courtesy. The questioner will usually recognize this reality also and will temper the follow-up accordingly.

Let's try an example:

Q: "Mr. Jones, why didn't your company bring in the early-response team from the state Department of Environmental Quality to help with this situation?"

Oops! You didn't even know the DEQ had an early-response team! You don't know what the questioner is talking about! So take a slow breath. Then do first things first by making your confession.

A: "I'm sorry, but I am drawing a blank on this question. If I have been briefed about a DEQ early-response team, it is not coming to mind right now."

Notice how this type of response allows for the truth of some confusion or a lapse in your memory? Often, a reference to "drawing a blank" or "not coming to mind" is more true than "I don't know." Why? Because you may have heard about the topic in another context and are simply not making the connection. Or you may have completely forgotten something today that you could have discussed at length yesterday.

Another option is to toss the ball back:

A: "Perhaps you can tell me more about this DEQ team, and I can try to answer your question."

Now the questioner becomes the questioned, and must make a decision about how to proceed. You will have a chance to think more about the topic while he decides and then does whatever he does.

There is a good chance that some explanation from the questioner will help you to make connections that allow you to respond appropriately. But remember the advice from earlier in this book. Don't make things up. Don't speculate. Don't guess. The follow-up information and the question you finally get may be answerable, but it also may just increase your confusion. If that happens, politely decline to answer because the truth is that you simply can't answer.

As said before, sometimes the most powerful response you can make is "I don't know."

The Truth

How about one more Truth?

That Truth is that you probably will not have absorbed much of what is in this little book after only one reading. Educational scientists tell us that it is difficult to retain more than just a few ideas from only one reading of a book. It is like learning to speak clearly about the truth; you have to do it more than once in order to do it right.

Reread the book a section at a time over the course of the next few days, trying to go through the whole book at least twice before your big moment. Each time you read it you will retain a little more of what is contained here. Please try to do the exercises, too. Do them more than once if possible.

Use the lessons of this book, and you will do fine when you find yourself in the hotseat.

Made in the USA
San Bernardino, CA
31 October 2017